Nevada

BY ANN HEINRICHS

Content Adviser: Jacqueline L. Clay, Nevada Historical Society, Reno, Nevada

Reading Adviser: Dr. Linda D. Labbo, Department of Reading Education, College of Education, The University of Georgia

COMPASS POINT BOOKS ✦ MINNEAPOLIS, MINNESOTA

Compass Point Books
3109 West 50th Street, #115
Minneapolis, MN 55410

Visit Compass Point Books on the Internet at *www.compasspointbooks.com*
or e-mail your request to *custserv@compasspointbooks.com*

On the cover: Red Rock Canyon

Photographs ©: Cheyenne Rouse/Visuals Unlimited, cover, 1; John Elk III, 3, 12, 20, 21, 28, 33, 36, 37, 41, 43 (top), 47, 48 (top); Alan Chapman/The Image Finders, 5, 42; Photo Network/Tom Campbell/ Boulanger, 6; Photo Network/Tom Campbell, 7, 23, 26; Scott T. Smith/Corbis, 8; Terry Donnely/Tom Stack & Associates, 9; Photo Network/TJ Florian, 10; Photo Network/Dunmire, 13; Corbis, 14; Hulton/Archive by Getty Images, 15, 17, 19; Stock Montage, 16; Bettmann/Corbis, 18; David Matherly/Visuals Unlimited, 24; Mark E. Gibson/Visuals Unlimited, 25, 35, 38; AP/Wide World Photos/Joe Cavaretta, 29; Alice Grulich-Jones/Omni-Photo Communications, 30; Laurence Fordyce; Eye Ubiquitous/Corbis, 31; Bachmann/The Image Finders, 32, 45; Marc Muench/Corbis, 34; Kennan Ward/Corbis, 40; Robesus, Inc., 43 (state flag); One Mile Up, Inc., 43 (state seal); Bill Leaman/The Image Finders, 44 (top left); John Gerlach/Tom Stack & Associates, 44 (middle left); Comstock, 44 (bottom right); Special Collections, University of Nevada-Reno Library, 46.

Editors: E. Russell Primm, Emily J. Dolbear, and Catherine Neitge
Photo Researcher: Svetlana Zhurkina
Photo Selector: Linda S. Koutris
Designer: The Design Lab
Cartographer: XNR Productions, Inc.

Library of Congress Cataloging-in-Publication Data
Heinrichs, Ann.
  Nevada / by Ann Heinrichs.
    p. cm. — (This land is your land)
  Summary: Introduces the geography, history, government, people, culture, and attractions of Nevada.
  Includes bibliographical references (p.) and index.
  ISBN 0-7565-0327-2
  1. Nevada—Juvenile literature. [1. Nevada.] I. Title. II. Series: Heinrichs, Ann. This land is your land.
F841.3.H45 2003
  979.3—dc21   2002010092

Table of Contents

Welcome to Nevada!

Robert Lindsey was a cowboy. He worked on a Nevada cattle ranch in the 1890s. "The place was so **lonesome,**" he said. "You'd go days and days there without seeing a human."

Much of Nevada is still "lonesome." Its empty deserts stretch on for miles. Nevada is full of natural beauty, too. It has colorful **canyons** as well as towering rocks. Sparkling Lake Tahoe sits high among snow-capped peaks.

Explorers and fur trappers began coming into Nevada in the 1820s. Then, in 1859, many more people discovered Nevada. Miners found rich deposits of silver and gold. Rough mining towns sprang up overnight. Over time, they became empty "ghost towns."

The 1930s brought a new promise of riches. **Gambling** was made legal in the state of Nevada. Las Vegas and Reno soon became the country's gambling capitals. Their bright lights lit up the desert sky.

▲ Nevada is home to great natural beauty, including lovely Lake Tahoe.

Today, Nevada is America's fastest-growing state. People find a lot to love there. Explore Nevada, and you're sure to love it, too!

The Colorado River forms the border between southern Nevada and Arizona.

Nevada is one of the nation's western states. It's big, too. Nevada is the seventh-largest state. Most of its borders are long, straight lines. To the north are Oregon and Idaho. California lies to the west. Utah and Arizona are on the east. Nevada's southeast corner is a wavy line. This is where the Colorado River forms Nevada's border with Arizona.

The Sierra Nevada mountains reach into western Nevada. Their higher peaks are snowcapped all

▲ **Theresa Lake, in Great Basin National Park, lies within the Sierra Nevada mountains.**

year round. In fact, that's how Nevada got its name. *Nevada* is a Spanish word, meaning "snow-covered."

▲ **The rock formation that gave Pyramid Lake its name**

Lake Tahoe perches high in the Sierra Nevada. Both California and Nevada share Lake Tahoe. Nearby are Reno, in a high desert valley, and Carson City, Nevada's state capital. To the north is **Pyramid** Lake, the state's largest lake. It's named for its tall, pointed rock island.

Most of Nevada lies in the Great Basin region. This area is shaped like a big basin, or bowl. More than one hundred fifty mountain ranges rise up there. Most of them run in a north–south direction.

Between the mountains are broad valleys and deserts. Some of these valleys have huge cattle ranches and farms. Others are dry, white lands called salt flats. They are the floors of lakes that dried up long ago. Nevada's sandy deserts stretch for miles. Strange **rock formations** rise up here and there.

▲ **Arch Rock is a natural sandstone formation in the Valley of Fire State Park.**

Nevada's major river is the Humboldt River. It runs through much of northern Nevada. Nevada's farms get water through **irrigation.** Dams are built on the rivers to hold the water back. Then **canals** carry water to the farms.

Some dams were built to make lakes. Hoover Dam on the Colorado River created Lake Mead. Both Nevada and Arizona share this lake. Nearby is Las Vegas, Nevada's largest city.

Deer and bears roam Nevada's forests. Mountain sheep scamper high on

▲ Hoover Dam was built in the 1930s. It is a national historic landmark.

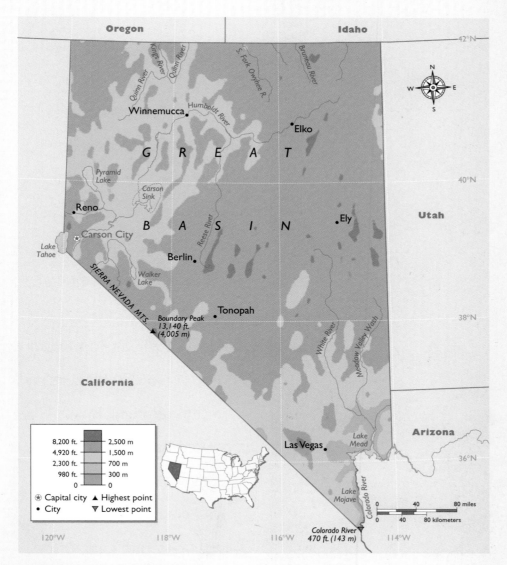

Oregon

Idaho

42°N

Kings River

Quinn River

Quinn River

S. Fork Owyhee R.

Bruneau River

Winnemucca

Humboldt River

Elko

G R E A T

Pyramid Lake

Carson Sink

40°N

Reno

Reese River

B A S I N

Ely

Carson City

Utah

Berlin

Lake Tahoe

SIERRA NEVADA MTS.

Walker Lake

Boundary Peak
13,140 ft.
(4,005 m)
▲

Tonopah

38°N

White River

Meadow Valley Wash

California

Las Vegas

Lake Mead

Arizona

36°N

Colorado River

Lake Mojave

Colorado River
470 ft. (143 m) ▼

0   40   80 miles
0   40   80 kilometers

120°W   118°W   116°W   114°W

▲ **A topographic map of Nevada**

rocky ledges. Coyotes, porcupines, and rabbits live in

Nevada, too. The deserts are home to snakes, lizards,

and tortoises.

▲ A bristlecone pine in Great Basin
National Park

Cactus and yucca plants grow in the desert. So do bushy plants such as sagebrush—the state flower. Nevada has two state trees. They are the piñon pine and the bristlecone pine. Piñon pines can grow on very rocky soil. Bristlecone pines are the oldest living things on Earth. Some are more than four thousand years old!

Nevada is hot and dry. It gets less rain and snow than any other state. Southern Nevada gets the hottest summers. Winters are coolest in the mountains. The Sierra Nevada is the wettest region. It gets both rain and snow.

▲ Hikers on a trail in Red Rock Canyon National Park

A Trip Through Time

People lived in Nevada thousands of years ago. By the 1800s, many American Indians had settled there. They moved from place to place depending on the weather and the food supply. The Shoshone and Paiute lived in the Great Basin. They gathered pine nuts and hunted. Their legends called them "children of the coyote."

The Washoe lived around Lake Tahoe. They hunted in the mountains and fished in the lakes. In the fall, they gathered pine nuts. The Mohave farmed along the Colorado River. Their songs told magical tales they learned in dreams.

▲ **Members of the Paiute tribe**

Nevada was part of a vast region claimed by Spain. This region passed to Mexico in 1821. American fur trappers soon discovered Nevada, however. An explorer named Peter Skene Ogden explored the Humboldt River Valley in the 1820s. Then trapper Jedediah Smith came through in 1826. A U.S. Army officer, John C. Frémont, arrived in 1843. His **scout** and guide was Kit Carson. They explored Nevada together for two years.

The United States won these lands from Mexico in 1848. At first, Nevada was part of Utah Territory, and members of the Mormon religion began to move in. They set up a trading post near Genoa in 1849. In 1861, Nevada became a separate territory.

▲ **Silver miners working the Comstock Lode**

The California gold rush began in 1849. Nevadans soon had riches of their own. Miners found silver and gold near Virginia City in 1859. This source of wealth was called the Comstock Lode.

▲ A silver mining town in the eastern Sierra Nevada

The news spread fast. Miners from around the world rushed in to make their fortunes. Mining towns seemed to spring up overnight. Some miners got rich, but most ended up empty-handed. When they left, the mining towns became "ghost towns."

Nevada became the thirty-sixth U.S. state in 1864. The U.S. Civil War (1861–1865) was still going on then. So Nevada called itself "Battle Born."

▲ Goldfield in 1902

In the early 1900s, a new mining rush began. Miners found silver in Tonopah and gold in Goldfield. They found copper in Ely, too. Meanwhile, farmers and ranchers struggled with Nevada's dry soil. The state began building dams for irrigation. Nevada made gambling legal in 1931. By the end of

World War II (1939–1945), gambling was a big business for the state.

Nevada's minerals were very useful during World War II. After the war, Nevada became important for other reasons. Nuclear weapons testing began there in 1951. Tests still go on in southern Nevada.

Today, many people are moving to Nevada. They enjoy its year-round warm weather. They also love its deserts, mountains, and lakes.

▲ Marines watch an atomic blast at the Yucca Flats during the early days of testing.

Nevada's state capitol in Carson City

Carson City grew up during the mining boom. It was named after a scout—Kit Carson. It has been Nevada's capital since 1861. Most state government offices are there.

Nevada's government works just like the U.S. government. It is divided into three branches—legislative, executive, and judicial. Having three branches is a good idea because it divides the governing power. This way, no branch has too much power.

The legislative branch

▲ The senate chamber is inside the State Legislative Building.

makes the state laws. Voters elect lawmakers to serve in Nevada's legislature. It has two houses, or parts. One is the twenty-one-member senate. The other is the forty-two-member assembly. Unlike the legislatures of most other states, Nevada's state legislature meets every other year.

The executive branch makes sure the state's laws are obeyed. Nevada's governor is the head of the executive branch. Voters choose a governor every four years. Voters

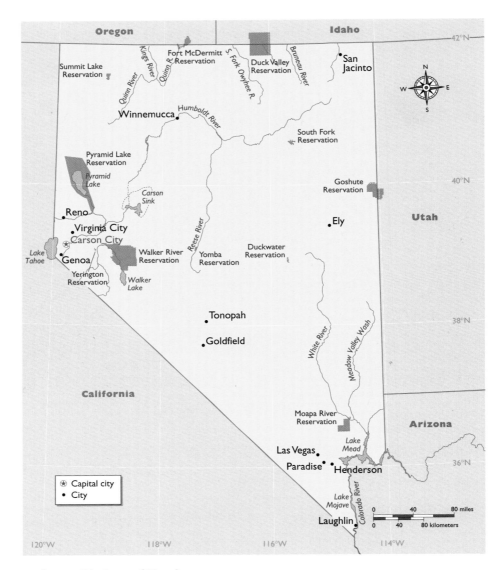

▲ **A geopolitical map of Nevada**

also elect several other executive officers. The governor chooses people to run various agencies. One such agency is the Gaming Control Board. It oversees the gambling **industry.**

Nevada's judges make up the judicial branch. They listen to cases in court. They then decide whether someone has broken the law. Nevada's highest court is the state supreme court. Districts, cities, and towns have courts, too.

Nevada is divided into seventeen counties. Voters elect commissioners to govern their counties in all counties except Carson City County. That county is governed by a board of supervisors. Cities and towns elect a mayor and a city council.

▲ **The Storey County Courthouse in Virginia City**

Nevadans at Work

Where does most of the nation's gold come from? If you guessed Nevada, you're right! Nevada is a world leader in gold, too. Only South Africa and Australia produce more gold. Nevada also leads the nation in silver, barite, and mercury.

▲ **Nevada produces more gold than any other state.**

▲ **Crowds of tourists visit Las Vegas every year.**

Although mining is important to Nevada, tourist services are the state's biggest industry. That's unusual. In most other states, manufacturing is the leader. Millions of tourists pour into Nevada every year. Many visit **casinos** in Las Vegas and Reno to try their luck at gambling. They also attend shows, ranging from singers to wild animals. Other visitors enjoy Nevada's lakes, deserts, or ski slopes. It takes a lot of service workers to help everyone!

▲ Real cowboys still work on ranches in Nevada.

Tourism keeps Nevada's economy healthy. Between 1990 and 2000, Nevada grew fast. The value of its goods and services more than doubled. In 2000, Nevada had the nation's fastest-growing economy.

Much of Nevada has a cowboy **culture.** Memories of the Old West are still alive. However, real cowboys work in Nevada, too. Most of the state's farmland is made up of cattle ranches. Cattle and calves are the leading farm products. Next in value is hay. Then comes milk and other dairy products. Nevadans also raise sheep, hogs, potatoes, and vegetables.

Nevada's factories make machines, food, concrete, and electrical goods. Printing plants turn out newspapers, magazines, and books. Packaged meat is the leading food product. Most of it goes to grocery stores. Some of it ends up as pet food.

Nevada is a big state with a small population. Just fewer than 2 million people live there. Imagine those people spread out evenly across Nevada. Each person would get almost twenty-seven football fields of land!

Nevada ranks only thirty-fifth in population among the states. But watch out! Nevada is growing every day. It's been the fastest-growing state for many years.

▲ **During the early silver-mining days, Austin was Nevada's second-largest city.**

▲ Members of the Western Shoshone tribe hold a protest in Mercury to oppose the building of a nuclear waste dump on Yucca Mountain. The federal government still plans to go ahead with construction during the next several years.

Outside of Las Vegas and Reno, Nevada is lightly settled. The majority of Nevadans live in the Las Vegas area.

Many Native Americans live on Nevada's Indian reservations. Most belong to Shoshone, Paiute, or Washoe groups. About one of every five Nevadans is **Hispanic, or Latino.** Another one of every fifteen residents is African-American.

▲ **Racing camels in the International Camel Races in Virginia City**

Festivals are a fun part of life in Nevada. For example, Virginia City holds International Camel Races in September! Camels are hard to control, though. Often the winner is any camel that finishes the race. Ostriches race there, too. The "ostrich drivers" ride behind the big birds in little carts.

January brings the Cowboy Poetry Gathering to Elko. Thousands of people come to celebrate cowboy culture. They hear poetry, dance, tell stories, and eat big steaks! Every June, the Reno Rodeo takes place. It has been called "the greatest outdoor rodeo in the world." Another spectacular cowboy event is the National Finals Rodeo. It is held in Las Vegas each December.

▲ **Riding a bucking bull is a popular event at the National Finals Rodeo.**

▲ **A Pueblo Indian boy in native dress dances at a festival.**

Henderson holds the Native American Arts Festival in April. It's a three-day event with dancing, food, and a crafts display. Many other cities also have Indian **powwows** and festivals.

Both Elko and Reno hold Basque festivals in summer. Basque people come from a region on the border of Spain and France. Their festivals celebrate Basque folk music, food, and sports.

Reno is also the site of Artown. This summer arts festival goes on for the entire month of July. It is one of the largest festivals for visual and performing arts in the United States.

▲ The colorful Dickinson Library at the University of Nevada in Las Vegas

Many writers told about life in Nevada and the West. Robert Laxalt wrote *Sweet Promised Land* (1957) about his father, a Basque immigrant. Walter Van Tilburg Clark wrote *The Ox-Bow Incident* (1940). It was made into a movie. Sarah Winnemucca Hopkins was a Paiute woman. She wrote *Life Among the Paiutes: Their Wrongs and Claims* (1883).

Authors Mark Twain and Bret Harte worked in Nevada. Both wrote for the *Territorial Enterprise* newspaper. Twain wrote about his Nevada adventures in *Roughing It* (1872).

The University of Nevada has two campuses. Reno's campus is called UNR. The Las Vegas campus is UNLV. The Running Rebels of UNLV are a top-notch basketball team.

▲ **Skiing on Ruby Mountain**

Nevada has no major-league sports teams. The people enjoy plenty of sports, however. Car racing, golf, skiing, fishing, and water sports are favorites.

Let's Explore Nevada!

Do aliens from outer space visit Earth? If you're curious, head out to state highway 375. It's called the **Extraterrestrial** Highway! Many people claim to have seen unidentified flying objects (UFOs) there.

Las Vegas has sights of a different kind. Bright neon lights flicker everywhere. Children may not enter the gambling areas. There is plenty for young people to do, though. There are pirate shows, circus acts, rides, and games.

▲ **An exciting sword fight at the MGM Grand Theme Park**

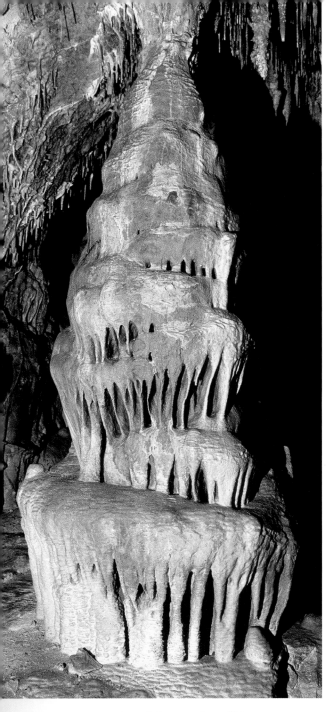

▲ One of the many incredible cave
formations in the Lehman Caves

Nearby is Lake Mead. You can ride a paddle-wheel boat on the lake. You can take a nature hike. You will pass colorful canyons, bighorn sheep, and tiny ground squirrels.

To the north is Great Basin National Park. There you'll see jagged peaks and ancient bristlecone pines. Then head underground to explore Lehman Caves. Awesome rock formations sparkle wherever you turn.

Long, lonely roads stretch across central Nevada. The deserts seem endless. Some "towns" consist of just a gas pump

▲ **Berlin, a ghost town and home to remains of ichthyosaurs**

and a little store. Others are ghost towns, such as Berlin. It is now famous as an ichthyosaur "graveyard." Ichthyosaurs are sea serpents from the dinosaur age. You can see one on display in Berlin.

How much would you weigh on the planet Jupiter? You'll find out at Reno's Fleischmann Planetarium. Reno's Animal Ark is a shelter for wild animals. Some are hurt, and others have lost their parents. Like Las Vegas, Reno is best known for gambling. You'll also find a lot of other things to do in Reno.

▲ Lake Tahoe, high in the Sierra Nevada, is a beautiful spot for nature lovers.

Lake Tahoe may well be the prettiest place in Nevada. It sits high in the Sierra Nevada mountains. Its clear waters change colors as the weather changes. You will love the view from the Tahoe Rim Trail. It runs along the mountain-tops above the lake.

In Carson City, near Lake Tahoe, you can tour the state capitol. The state museum has a full-size model of a ghost town!

Nevada's most famous mining town is Virginia City. Its population shrank from thirty thousand to about one thousand. You can still stroll down the old wooden sidewalks, though. A train carries you up to Gold Hill.

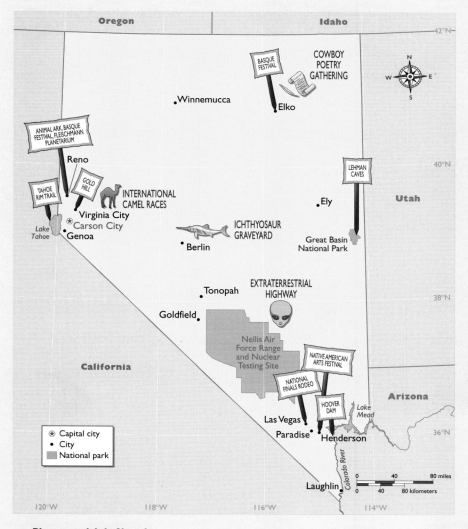

▲ **Places to visit in Nevada**

▲ This rock formation rising over Pyramid Lake looks like an old woman and a basket.

Pyramid Lake lies within a Paiute Indian reservation. A rock island called Stone Mother rises up in the lake. It looks like a woman sitting beside a basket. Paiute folklore says Stone Mother is the mother of all people. Her Paiute children stayed home but she missed her other children and cried so much that her tears formed Pyramid Lake.

Stone Mother is just one of many reasons to visit Nevada. Whether you enjoy natural beauty or exciting attractions, you'll never run out of things to do in this wonderful state.

Important Dates

1776 Francisco Garcés may be the first European in Nevada.

1821 Nevada becomes part of Mexico.

1826 Jedediah Smith is the first American to cross Nevada.

1843– 1845 Kit Carson and John C. Frémont explore Nevada.

1848 Nevada becomes U.S. land after the Mexican War (1846–1848).

1859 Silver is discovered in Virginia City. Mining rush begins.

1864 Nevada becomes the thirty-sixth state on October 31.

1874 The University of Nevada opens in Elko. (It moved to Reno in 1885.)

1909 Gambling is outlawed in Nevada.

1931 Gambling is made legal.

1936 Boulder Dam (now Hoover Dam) is completed.

1951 Nuclear weapons testing begins in southern Nevada.

1963 The U.S. Supreme Court settles Colorado River water rights.

1980 State law protects Lake Tahoe from pollution.

1986 Great Basin National Park becomes Nevada's first national park.

2001 The state legislature approves a Nevada Protection Fund to resist the federal government's construction of a nuclear waste dump at Yucca Mountain.

Glossary

canals—human-made waterways

canyons—deep, narrow valleys with steep sides, often with a stream or river flowing through

casinos—buildings used for gambling activities

culture—a group of people who share beliefs, customs, and a way of life

extraterrestrial—a creature from outer space

gambling—playing games of chance for money

Hispanic, or Latino—people of Mexican, South American, or other Spanish speaking cultures

industry—a business or trade

irrigation—a way of bringing water to fields through canals

powwows—Native American gatherings for meetings or ceremonies

lonesome—lonely

pyramid—a solid, triangle-shaped figure

rock formations—rocks formed into unusual shapes

scout—an explorer

Did You Know?

★ Ichthyosaur, the state fossil, was a giant sea serpent. It grew as long as 60 feet (18 m).

★ Nevadans used camels as pack animals in the 1800s.

★ Hard hats for construction workers were invented for the workers who built Hoover Dam, completed in 1936.

★ Nevada's Native Americans used more than three hundred plants for medicines and teas.

★ Nevada has more mountain ranges than any other state.

★ A rare fish called the cui-ui lives in Pyramid Lake.

At a Glance

State capital: Carson City

State motto: All for Our Country

State nicknames: Silver State, Sagebrush State, Battle-Born State

Statehood: October 31, 1864; thirty-sixth state

Area: 110,567 square miles (286,367 sq km); **rank:** seventh

Highest point: Boundary Peak, 13,140 feet (4,005 m) above sea level

Lowest point: Along the Colorado River in Clark County, 470 feet (143 m) above sea level

Highest recorded temperature: 125°F (52°C) at Laughlin on June 29, 1994

Lowest recorded temperature: −50°F (−46°C) at San Jacinto on January 8, 1937

Average January temperature: 30°F (−1°C)

Average July temperature: 73°F (23°C)

Population in 2000: 1,998,257; **rank:** thirty-fifth

Largest cities in 2000: Las Vegas (478,434), Paradise (186,070), Reno (180,480), Henderson (175,381)

Factory products: Foods, concrete, printed material, electronics

Farm products: Beef cattle, sheep, hay

Mining products: Gold, silver, diatomite

State flag: Nevada's state flag has a blue background. At the upper left is a silver star. Above the star is a banner reading "Battle Born." That was Nevada's original nickname. It refers to Nevada's becoming a state during the Civil War. Under the star is the name "Nevada" and two sprigs of sagebrush. They represent the state flower.

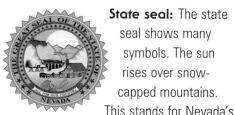

State seal: The state seal shows many symbols. The sun rises over snow-capped mountains. This stands for Nevada's beautiful scenery. A train chugs by next to a telegraph line. This stands for Nevada's place between the nation's Midwest and West. A mine represents minerals. A plow, sickle, and bundle of wheat stand for farming. At the bottom is the state motto, "All for Our Country."

State abbreviations: Nev. (traditional); NV (postal)

State Symbols

State bird: Mountain bluebird

State flower: Sagebrush

State trees: Single-leaf piñon and bristle-cone pine

State animal: Desert bighorn sheep

State reptile: Desert tortoise

State fish: Lahontan cutthroat trout

State grass: Indian ricegrass

State metal: Silver

State rock: Sandstone

State precious gemstone: Black fire opal and turquoise

State semiprecious gemstone: Turquoise

State artifact: Tule duck decoy

State fossil: Ichthyosaur

Making Alien Cookies

UFO fans say Nevada is the alien capital of the world!

Makes about thirty-six cookies.

INGREDIENTS:

2/3 cup butter or margarine, softened

3/4 cup sugar

1 teaspoon baking powder

1/8 teaspoon salt

1 teaspoon vanilla extract

1 egg

2 cups flour

1 can chocolate frosting

DIRECTIONS:

Make sure an adult helps with the hot stove. Preheat oven to 325°. Put butter or margarine in a bowl. Mix in sugar, baking powder, and salt. Add vanilla and egg. Mix well. Slowly stir in flour. Chill dough in refrigerator for 1 hour. Roll out dough 1/4 inch thick on a floured board. Cut out 3-inch alien heads. Cut out circles with a cookie cutter. Shape each head into an alien head by pushing on the edges to make a pointy chin. Place on nonstick cookie sheet. Bake for 7 to 8 minutes. Use the frosting to draw huge eyes and a tiny mouth.

"Home Means Nevada"

Words and music by Bertha Raffetto

Way out in the land of the setting sun,
Where the wind blows wild and free,
There's a lovely spot, just the only one
That means home sweet home to me.
If you follow the old Kit Carson trail,
Until desert meets the hills,
Oh you certainly will agree with me,
It's the place of a thousand thrills.

Chorus:
Home means Nevada, Home means the hills,
Home means the sage and the pines.
Out by the Truckee's silvery rills,
Out where the sun always shines,
There is the land that I love the best,
Fairer than all I can see.
Right in the heart of the golden west
Home means Nevada to me.

Whenever the sun at the close of day,
Colors all the western sky,
Oh my heart returns to the desert grey
And the mountains tow'ring high.
Where the moonbeams play in shadowed glen,
With the spotted fawn and doe,
All the livelong night until morning light,
Is the loveliest place I know.

Eva Bertrand Adams (1908–1991) was the director of the U.S. Mint (1961–1969). Before that, she taught at the University of Nevada in Reno.

Andre Agassi (1970–) is a tennis champion who was born in Las Vegas. He lives there still.

Kit Carson (1809–1868) was the scout who guided John C. Frémont's exploration of Nevada. Carson City is named for him.

Walter Van Tilburg Clark (1909–1971) was a writer. His novel *The Ox-Bow Incident* (1940) was made into a movie. Clark was born in Maine and grew up in Reno.

Henry Comstock (1820–1870) claimed the gold and silver deposits that became the Comstock Lode.

Dat-so-la-lee (1829–1925) was a Washoe Indian woman, the last of the famed Washoe basket weavers. Her baskets were known for their beauty and symbolism.

Sarah Winnemucca Hopkins (1844?–1891) was a Paiute translator and author. She worked for peace and Indian rights. Hopkins wrote *Life Among the Paiutes: Their Wrongs and Claims* (1883).

Paul Laxalt (1922–) was Nevada's governor (1967–1971) and U.S. senator (1974–1987). He also managed Ronald Reagan's presidential campaigns in 1976 and 1980.

Robert Laxalt (1923–2001) was Paul Laxalt's brother and a writer who composed books on Basque history and culture. Laxalt (pictured above left) also wrote *Sweet Promised Land,* the story of a journey he and his immigrant father took to Basque country in the 1950s.

John William Mackay (1831–1902) grew rich on the Comstock Lode. He founded a bank and telegraph companies. Mackay was born in Ireland. The Mackay School of Mines at the University of Nevada is named after him.

Pat Nixon (1912–1993) was the wife of President Richard Nixon. She was born Thelma Catherine Ryan in Ely.

Mark Twain (1835–1910) was a famous author. His book *Roughing It* (1872) told of his adventures in Nevada. He was born in Missouri as Samuel Clemens.

Wovoka (1856?–1932), a Paiute Indian and religious leader, started the Ghost Dance religion. He used the name Jack Wilson. Wovoka was considered a prophet among his people.

Want to Know More?

At the Library

Joseph, Paul. *Nevada.* Minneapolis:
Abdo & Daughters, 1998.

Marsh, Carole. *The Hard to Believe but
True! Nevada History, Mystery, Trivia,
Legend, Lore and More.* Decatur, Ga.:
Gallopade, 1990.

Sirvaitis, Karen. *Nevada.* Minneapolis:
Lerner, 1992.

Stefoff, Rebecca. *Nevada.* Tarrytown,
N.Y.: Benchmark Books, 2001.

On the Web

Nevada

http://www.silver.state.nv.us/
For the state web site, with information
on Nevada's government, economy,
and services

Nevada Kids Page

http://dmla.clan.lib.nv.us/docs/kids/
For lots of fun facts from the Nevada
State Library and Archives

Nevada Tourism

http://www.travelnevada.com
For a look at Nevada's events, activities,
and sights

Through the Mail

Nevada Commission on Economic Development

108 East Proctor Street
Carson City, NV 89701
For information on Nevada's economy

Nevada Commission on Tourism

401 North Carson Street
Carson City, NV 89701
For information on travel and interesting
sights in Nevada

On the Road

Nevada Historical Society

1650 North Virginia Street
Reno, NV 89503
775/688-1190
To visit Nevada's oldest museum and
learn more about the history of the state

Nevada State Capitol

101 North Carson Street
Carson City, NV 89701
775/687-4810
To visit Nevada's capitol

Nevada State Museum

600 North Carson Street
Carson City, NV 89701
775/687-4810
To learn more about Nevada's natural
history, native peoples, and frontier days

Index

About the Author

Ann Heinrichs grew up in Fort Smith, Arkansas, and lives in Chicago. She is the author of more than eighty books for children and young adults on Asian, African, and U.S. history and culture. Ann has also written numerous newspaper, magazine, and encyclopedia articles. She is an award-winning martial artist, specializing in t'ai chi empty-hand and sword forms.

Ann has traveled widely throughout the United States, Africa, Asia, and the Middle East. In exploring each state for this series, she rediscovered the people, history, and resources that make this a great land, as well as the concerns we share with people around the world.